FROM ORDINARY TO EXTRAORDINARY

HOW TO RE-IMAGINE YOURSELF
& RE-DEFINE WHAT IS POSSIBLE

JESPER LOWGREN

From my heart to yours

ABOUT THE AUTHOR

Jesper Lowgren is a philosopher and thought-leader who consults to corporate CEOs on how to transform their leadership team and organisation for the digital world.

He is the author of *ON PURPOSE: The Path to Extraordinary Business Transformation*, where he introduces a groundbreaking framework and process for transforming an organisation, based on values and purpose.

Jesper loves everything digital, and is a pioneer in building and commercialising online communities. In Australia he has created three number 1 online communities in three different industries, connecting more than 100,000 people to what they are passionate about.

Jesper is married to artist Melissa Mladin-Lowgren, has three ragdoll cats, and lives in Sydney, Australia.

PREFACE

This book introduces radical new concepts – new, because they didn't exist before, and radical, because they are very simple. Indeed, they are so simple, your mind will struggle to accept them.

How to introduce these concepts raised a challenge for me. Ultimately, I decided to write the book in a question and answer format. I believe this allowed its content to be probed and scrutinised, and be challenged on anything and everything that doesn't pass the common-sense test.

No one scrutinises or challenges me more than my greatest critic and sceptic, my wife, Melissa. And it is Melissa who has contributed a majority of the questions this book attempts to answer.

The remaining questions are audience questions from workshops, seminars and presentations. Ultimately, I hope these questions echo any that you may have as you read through the book, and allow you to scrutinise the content and make changes in your own life.

Jesper Lowgren
Sydney, Australia

www.jesperlowgren.com
twitter: @jesperlowgren
linkedin: au.linkedin.com/in/jesperlowgren

First published in 2015 by Jesper Lowgren

© Jesper Lowgren 2015
The moral rights of the author have been asserted

All rights reserved. Except as permitted under the *Australian Copyright Act 1968* (for example, a fair dealing for the purposes of study, research, criticism or review), no part of this book may be reproduced, stored in a retrieval system, communicated or transmitted in any form or by any means without prior written permission. All inquiries should be made to the author.

National Library of Australia Cataloguing-in-Publication entry:
Creator: Lowgren, Jesper, author
Title: From ordinary to extraordinary
ISBN: 9780994472557 (paperback)
Subjects: Self-actualization (Psychology)
              Motivation (Psychology)
              Success – Psychological aspects
              Creative ability
              Resourcefulness
Dewey number: 158.1

Text design and book production by Michael Hanrahan Publishing
Cover design by Michael Hoffmann
Illustrations by Jesper Lowgren

Disclaimer
The material in this publication is of the nature of general comment only, and does not represent professional advice. It is not intended to provide specific guidance for particular circumstances and it should not be relied on as the basis for any decision to take action or not take action on any matter which it covers. Readers should obtain professional advice where appropriate, before making any such decision. To the maximum extent permitted by law, the author and publisher disclaim all responsibility and liability to any person, arising directly or indirectly from any person taking or not taking action based on the information in this publication.

CONTENTS

INTRODUCTION 1

PART I: PREPARING THE MIND 5

1. Everything you believe comes true 7
2. Your subconscious makes all important choices 11
3. Think differently, or do differently 16
4. The point of simplicity 21
5. Choose extraordinary, not ordinary 27

PART II: IGNITE THE HEART 33

6. Laugh at your thoughts 35
7. Language of the heart 43
8. You are only your values 48
9. Do what you love doing 53
10. The art of charisma 58

PART III: SET YOUR GOALS 67

11. Knowing your one true goal 69
12. Understand goals and brain chemistry 75
13. SEISMIC goals that rock your inner 81
14. Create your SEISMIC goal 87
15. The art of clarity 95

PART IV: CREATE THE EXTRAORDINARY   101

16. There is no Plan B   103
17. Find what is uniquely yours, and only yours   109
18. Find your project   114
19. Get shit done   120
20. The art of manifestation   126

CONCLUSION   134

INTRODUCTION

This book is unique.

It is not a regurgitation or a copy. It contains no plagiarism.

What this book does contain is a blueprint for creating a radically different life.

It is a game-changer, a circuit breaker – or whatever you choose to call it. This book will change everything, or nothing, or any shade in-between. How it changes you is up to you. You choose. You are always in the driver's seat.

That's a big promise. What qualifies you to write a book like this?

What qualifies anyone to write anything that is unique?

You cannot learn *unique* from someone else, because then whatever you've learnt is no longer unique. Unique means there can be one, and only *one*. So if you cannot learn it, you must already know it.

This uniqueness is often referred to as your unique *gifts and abilities* – things that only you know, and things only you can do.

Developing your gifts and abilities is a key theme in this book, because when you connect with them, *extraordinary* things happen.

From this perspective, I am uniquely qualified to write this book, because it is a direct result of *my* unique gifts and abilities.

So I should just trust you, in other words?

No. Absolutely not.

You need to trust in yourself, and in your common sense.

This book espouses clarity and simplicity – if something cannot be understood, and if it does not pass the common-sense test, it is not right for you.

This book is not about *the* truth; it is about *a* truth.

You are not telling the truth?

There is no such thing. If there were, everyone would have accepted it. Instead, everyone is unique, and everyone has a unique experience of life, and so a unique interpretation of truth.

What I write about is *one* truth, one of many, but one that holds the potential for changing everything, if you choose to embrace it.

This truth has a purpose. It means to set you alive, help you reset your life compass, and set you free to *be* and *do* extraordinary things.

Aren't you just beating your own drum here?

If I am to help you come alive, I must be alive myself.

If I am to help you shine your light, I must first shine my own.

I walk my talk, and lead by example. How else can I be authentic? How else can you trust me?

Is my approach inspirational or full of self-importance? You read the book and decide!

And why are you doing it? What are you trying to sell me?

What I sell is *choice*. The choice of becoming extraordinary. The choice of doing extraordinary things and creating extraordinary outcomes.

My purpose is to help you become extraordinary. To help you come alive. To help you make a *real* difference, to yourself and others.

And by living my purpose, I come alive.

Can you tell me more about the choice?

The first choice is to accept your uniqueness, and the key implication this acceptance creates: *you can do things no-one else can do.* You may not yet know what these things are, but you intuitively know it to be true.

This choice is critical. If you fundamentally believe you are the same as everyone else, little in this book will make sense.

But if you believe in your own uniqueness, you must also believe in mine.

And with this uniqueness in common, I want to take you on a unique and extraordinary journey, to help you find your *extraordinary*.

Are you ready?

PART I
PREPARING THE MIND

Logic will take you from A to B.
Imagination will take you everywhere.

ALBERT EINSTEIN

1. EVERYTHING YOU BELIEVE COMES TRUE

Everything you believe comes true.

I say it again. Everything you believe comes true.

You may find this hard to take in, perhaps even impossible. But I will show you.

It is a bit hard to believe – some things I believe come true, perhaps, but not everything. That is impossible.

I agree. I am not going to argue it, because I cannot.

But I will paint a different picture, with a new perspective. One that is radical in its simplicity, and is designed to change everything, if you choose to let it.

Please let me start by asking you a question. What belief do you hold that has not come true?

I thought I was going to marry a prince.

Perhaps you did.

I mean a rich one!

That may still come true. Try again.

Tell me your definition of a belief first.

A *belief* is different to a *want*. A belief is *automatic* and something you do without thinking. Once you stop and think about what you want, you create not a belief but a conscious *choice*.

Can you give me an example?

Yes – one that is confronting for everyone. The belief is … *I need to be right.*

This belief is very persuasive, and explains your initial reaction to defend yourself when challenged. You are taught to be right, not wrong.

This belief is responsible for much of your evolution. And it seems so reasonable, especially considering the opposite. Why would you want to be wrong, when you can be right?

Yes, why would you want to? Why are we even having this conversation?

If you think you are always right, satisfying as that thought may be, how can you evolve? How can new insights and understanding come your way? Not insights that support what you already think, but those that challenge your thinking and allow you to evolve.

And this is a crossroad.

If you are not willing to challenge how you think, and be open to being wrong, you won't evolve.

You are saying I should leave the possibility open of being wrong? About my beliefs? What about you? What if I am right and you are wrong?

Great! I'll happily be wrong. Or right. It makes no difference.

My purpose for writing this book is to give you a choice. A choice that holds the potential to change everything.

To help you make this choice, I hope to give you a new perspective, a new angle and, if it looks attractive enough, the tools and processes so that you can choose it for yourself.

But whether you choose it, or not, is up to you. I hold no attachment to how you choose. My purpose is simply to give you a new choice, one you did not have before.

Right or wrong does not figure into it. It is about what truly makes you come alive – and be extraordinary, and do extraordinary things.

This is not an *if*, but a *how*, and this book is about the *how*. If you are willing to examine a few of your current beliefs, you will take the first steps on an incredible journey.

You have me interested. But let me just clarify please: you have no ulterior motive? Nothing cult-like?

I have no ulterior motive, other than giving you a new perspective, and a new choice.

The only cult I am part of is the cult of *common sense*.

2. YOUR SUBCONSCIOUS MAKES ALL IMPORTANT CHOICES

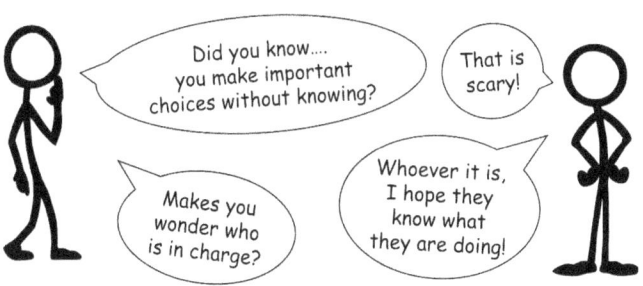

A belief is an automatic choice. It is the choice of *one*, and a choice you make automatically, because you have no choice.

Automatic choices are made in your *subconscious*, the area of your consciousness you are not fully aware of.

Stop and think about this for a moment ...

You are making choices you are not aware of.

And not just minor, insignificant choices, but the important ones – choices about *creativity* and *confidence*, to name a few.

Perhaps this makes you wonder who is really in charge here – you or something else?

It doesn't sound very good when you put it that way. Can you give me an example of one of these subconscious choices and beliefs?

That is difficult, because what lies in your subconscious is hidden.

Does that mean I cannot change it?

You can, but it is not straightforward. You cannot see into your subconscious, and what you cannot see, you cannot choose.

But beliefs can be replaced, as long as you are clear on what you want to replace them with. Using this approach, you can replace old beliefs with new beliefs you choose.

I don't think I can name a specific belief.

That is right, because the belief lives in your subconscious mind. This doesn't matter, however, because you don't need to know the old belief – you only need to know the new one you want to replace it with. This concept will be expanded throughout the book.

For now, let's start with one of your most important beliefs: your belief around *success*. This belief is created in childhood, and is reinforced through school, work and social experiences.

Beliefs on how to create success vary and come in many forms, such as:

- copying successful people
- working hard
- being lucky, or in the right place at the right time.

Creating success through copying successful people is a very popular belief, and a whole book genre in itself. Many of these books are good, and they can create good results.

That is a good point. Do we need any more?

You have two kinds of potential.

One is the potential you share with everyone else, achieved by copying what others have already done. I call this the *lowest common denominator of success*.

Your other potential is radically different. It is not limited by others. It does not follow someone else's footsteps, but creates a new path entirely.

This path leads straight into the heart of *your* potential. It empowers you to apply everything you have, including your unique gifts and abilities, to create your own extraordinary success.

I call this the *highest uncommon denominator of success*, because this success is unique to you.

That is quite a claim.

Well, there is more ...

The lowest common denominator of success is determined by something *external* to you - that is, something on the outside. Something you have no control over. Because it is shared by many, it has to be this way - it cannot be changed by one.

The highest uncommon denominator of success, on the other hand, is *internal*, and is something you can learn to master and have full control over.

But to choose this path, you need to look on the inside, not the outside. You cannot learn it from someone else.

So how can I learn it if no-one can tell me?

You already know it.

This book is about outlining the process to help you remember. Only you know what to look for, but working out where to look can be described.

But looking in a different place requires different *thinking*. If you could find this place with your current thinking, you would have done so already.

How you *think* is controlled by your *beliefs*. By changing how you think, you change a belief.

Why is this important?

You are aware of your thoughts, so they are easier to change. You can target specific thoughts, and force a change in your thinking pattern.

These changes are radical. What you believe comes true, so when you change a belief, you change your life.

3. THINK DIFFERENTLY, OR DO DIFFERENTLY

Your journey doesn't start with *doing* anything. You are already busy doing things – and quite possibly busy doing too many things. Instead, your journey starts with *not* doing.

My journey starts with 'not doing'? That sounds somewhat esoteric. I was hoping for something a little more practical.

You mean you'd like something you can go out and *do* immediately? You want more *doing*?

What you need is to stop, take time out, and reflect. And what does that have to do with extraordinary? Everything, because when you are in the state of *reflection,* you are also in the state of *reception*, and this state is a precondition for new *thinking*.

So what do I do? Sit cross-legged? Chant an om mantra? Perform a sacrifice to the gods?

Perhaps later.

For now, your first action in the journey is to stop, and be *open* to something new.

This is not an easy concept to initially come to terms with, because it raises the possibility you don't know something, or you are wrong about something.

But being open to something new is critical, because doing so challenges your existing thinking.

> *More doing with the same thinking leads to the ordinary. More doing with different thinking leads to the extraordinary.*

This simple concept explains why so many actions and plans fail. Apply this concept to your own life, and contemplate what has worked, and what hasn't. You will find that everything successful was preceded by different thinking, and actions that were less successful were preceded by the same thinking.

This is a critical success factor in becoming extraordinary. If you want to make an extraordinary change in your life, and do extraordinary things, you must first think differently, compared to how you think now.

But how do I think differently? I mean, nothing I have learnt has prepared me for something like this.

To think *differently* is not an easy concept if you have been brought up in the Western world. Western education systems are largely based on historical or scientific knowledge, culminating in conclusions that are taught as truths.

But another aspect to truth is not based on external knowledge. This truth is based on your *inner* knowledge, or *knowing*. This is what you *know* to be true, even if you haven't learned it.

You find this truth by asking the *right* questions, because no answer is better than the question.

Unfortunately, Western culture and thinking is largely based on Greek and Greek-inspired philosophy and thinking.

Wonderful as these foundations may be, they do not force us to ask meaningful questions, or encourage us to discover our own uniqueness, and what makes us *different from*, versus *similar to*, others.

Do philosophies that focus on discovering our own uniqueness really exist? I don't think I have ever heard of one.

You probably have, but they are unlike what we have in the West, and are not well understood here. Examples include Taoism, traditional Chinese medicine, and Kabbalah.

I collectively refer to these approaches as *Eastern philosophy*. They are fundamentally different from Western philosophy, to the point they cannot be compared because they come from opposite directions:

- Western philosophy is about *understanding* and *knowledge*. It is fact-based and comes from the *bottom-up* to build insights or draw conclusions, often in the context of what is *right* or *wrong*. It values reason, logic and rationality.

- Eastern philosophy is about *experience* and *knowing*. It is experiential and comes from the *top-down*, focusing on creating the best life experience. It values passion, inspiration and joy.

Oh. That sounds complex.

Quite the opposite. Eastern philosophy is based on *simplicity*. It doesn't try to prove anything. It doesn't try to be right, because it really doesn't care, insofar as it affects your life experience for better or worse.

Eastern philosophy provides a radically different lens on life, through which things appear different.

This approach helps you change your Western thinking, by removing complexities, judgements and other interferences that create a fog within which you cannot see clearly, and within which the extraordinary is always hidden.

4. THE POINT OF SIMPLICITY

To think differently is no longer a luxury but a necessity, because you live in a *complex* world.

And to make the situation worse, change is *accelerating*, increasing complexity.

But change itself is not necessarily complex to understand if we break it down into two simple aspects:

- External change, which is happening outside of you. You have no control over this change.

- Internal change, which relates to your internal ability to respond to external change. You have full control of this change.

Humans normally resist change, which causes real problems and disruption when external change is increasing.

Yes, I can relate to that. Things are changing more quickly. But how do I know if internal and external changes are in balance, or not?

You know an imbalance exists when you struggle to keep up – when you are juggling many balls already, and new ones keep coming.

I call this the *change race*, and it is possibly your most important race ever, because if you fall behind, you lose your relevance.

You cannot win the change race, because you cannot outrun it. Put simply, you cannot do anything.

Then what is the point of this book?

I want to give you a different choice – the choice of creating and running in your own change race. But to do that you need *think* differently.

But what does that mean? To think differently?

In this context, it means creating your own race. And in a race, like in any game or competition, you need rules.

This gives you two options. You can:

- adopt someone else's rules

- create your own.

All things being equal, I assume you want to create your own rules. This means you need to learn something new, something no-one can teach you.

No-one can teach you because you already know it. This something is not learned from external knowledge, but from your inner knowing, which has always been part of you.

This is why new and different thinking is needed, because this thinking allows you to access your inner knowing.

I have to say I am struggling with this concept. What you say makes finding your inner knowing sound impossible.

Yes, because you are used to learning from *knowledge*, rather than from *knowing*. Whereas knowledge is an amalgamation of other's truths, *knowing* is your own.

Knowledge is freely available to everyone. And when you rely on knowledge to differentiate yourself in the world, you compete against everyone else.

When you rely on knowing, you stand out because it is your own. This knowing cannot be copied.

> *Your knowing makes you unique.*
> *Your knowledge makes you compete.*

I cannot tell you what your *knowing* is. No-one can. But I know how to undertake the journey of discovering it, and can show you how you can discover yours.

But what makes knowing so special? What difference does it make?

Knowing empowers, because it connects your dots, and gives you a vastly greater understanding of yourself.

It is your own unique formula for extraordinary success.

This all sounds great but how do I do find it?

Finding your knowing begins by first accepting that nothing extraordinary happens in a complex world. Or in a world where you juggle too many balls.

Put simply, in a complex world everything is unclear. Clarity comes from simplicity.

But not all simplicity is equal, because sometimes *simplicity* is mistaken for *simplified*. Consider the following:

- Simplified is about going back to the previous iteration(s) of complexity.
- Simplicity is about going back to the very beginning, the genesis, before any complexity was created.

The difference in clarity these two approaches provide is game-changing. The two approaches create two uniquely different outlooks on life, and two different takes on what is possible.

Back-to-the-dot theory describes how this works. This theory is a key concept in this book, and will be referenced extensively throughout the remaining chapters.

Back-to-the-dot theory

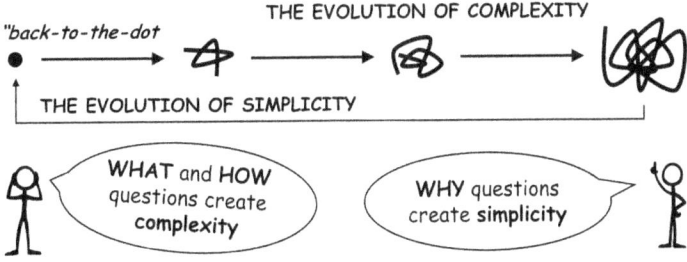

To understand simplicity, you need to know how complexity is created.

Everything starts with something singular, something simple, that then takes form. Even the universe started from a singular particle, prior to the Big Bang.

You are no different. Everything you do starts with something singular, such as a single *thought* or *intention*.

If you choose to do something with this thought, it grows and takes form, and as it grows, more complexity is created.

But as complexity grows, you can gradually lose sight of the original intention, or purpose, behind WHAT you are doing, and WHY you are doing it.

That makes sense but I am confused. How is this connected to some of the other concepts you've discussed, like new thinking?

Back-to-the-dot theory explains how to change your thinking.

WHAT and HOW questions don't challenge the existing paradigm, or your existing thinking, and hence cannot be used. Indeed, the WHAT and HOW questions create complexity in the first place.

It is the WHY question that challenges and, if asked repeatedly, brings you back to simplicity, and to what is the *most* important thought or intention. Back to *your dot*.

I have asked the WHY question many times, but never experienced anything you are talking about.

There is an art to asking WHY questions. Asked correctly, they eventually become personal, because they lead to what is most important and meaningful to you.

How to ask them is a theme addressed throughout this book, allowing you to go increasingly deeper within.

This is important, because *extraordinary* originates from what is *most* important and meaningful to you.

5. CHOOSE EXTRAORDINARY, NOT ORDINARY

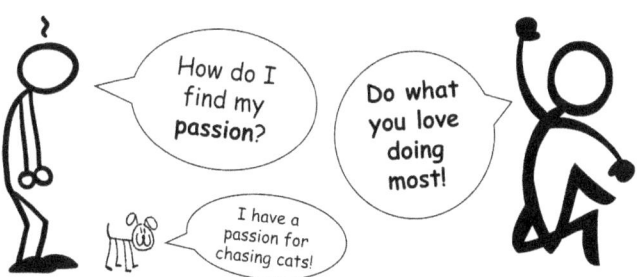

This is the end of the first part of the book. And like all endings, it also leads to a new beginning.

That new beginning rests on four key insights from the previous chapters:

- Everything you believe comes true. If you want a different outcome, you need to change a belief.

- You are not aware of your beliefs, and hence you cannot choose them directly.

- To change your beliefs, you need to first *think* differently. If you only *do* differently, you simply repeat old patterns and mistakes.

- You can change how you think by seeking *simplicity* over *complexity*, by continuously ask the WHY question, until you are back at the atomic simplicity.

I think I understand what you are saying – that I am naturally empowered to make any choices I want in life. But I am still not clear on what exactly my extraordinary choice is?

That's because we haven't talked about it yet.

To have jumped straight in would have been counterproductive, because your mind would have raised too many objections. The previous four chapters have prepared the mind for what is coming. Now we've done that, the time has come to describe exactly how to choose *extraordinary*.

We will use *back-to-the-dot* theory, apply it to *success* and *extraordinary*, and reduce them to three atomic levers, or switches.

By changing these levers, in the right sequence, *you* decide your setting of extraordinary and success.

Are you telling me I only need to do or change three things to be extraordinary? So what are they?

Yes, you only need to do three things to guarantee success and be extraordinary. The rest of this book is about describing these three levers and, most importantly, *how you can set your levers*, because your setting is unique.

Although all three levers are equally important, success and being extraordinary always start with the first lever, which is *passion*.

Passion is a true game changer. It holds the potential to change *everything*, because it bypasses your *mind*, and hence your entire belief system. This opens the door for adding new beliefs, replacing whatever is old and no longer serving you.

Passion is powerful because it comes from the heart. It is the fuel and energy that supercharges your *presence* and *charisma*.

It is unique and cannot be faked, and hence creates instant trust. Because it comes from the heart, passion connects directly with the hearts of others, especially those around you.

Being passionate is not always good. I have heard of situations where passion and passionate people have led to bad outcomes.

Keep in mind that enthusiasm and drive, and having high energy and a strong personality are not the same as passion. Anything that originates from the ego will create conflict of some kind because, ultimately, the ego sees its own win as most important.

But what you have heard from others isn't important. This is about *you*, and the choices *you* make and the beliefs *you* hold.

The passion I speak of does not come from the ego, but from the heart. Put simply, it is the *doorway* between *ordinary* and *extraordinary*. All extraordinary people have *passion* in common. They are passionate about different things, but they are all passionate.

Passion does not guarantee success,
but you cannot be truly successful without it.

You may not yet know what you are passionate about, but that's okay. Part II outlines how to discover your passion, and how to use it.

Okay, I can go along with that for now. What is the next step or lever?

You must have a *goal* – and just not any goal. It needs to be *the* goal. And *the* goal is the goal that *holistically* meets what you *want*, *need* and *value*.

This is important, because goals often focus on the *outcome*, neglecting the *journey*. But what is the point of achieving an outcome, if doing so creates misery?

And many people, once they have reached a goal, immediately create a new goal, and a new path of misery to achieve it.

How do I set the right goal?

It is simple. Your goal needs to be something you want to achieve, and something you are *passionate* about.

Quite possibly, you don't know what your true goal is yet, but that's okay. Part III outlines a process for discovering and defining your goal.

Interesting, that all makes sense. What is the third lever?

Your unique gifts and abilities.

They are the things only you can do, and no-one else. They are your special tools, the ones you can use to create your extraordinary masterpiece.

You probably don't know what your unique gifts and abilities are. Most don't, because certain things need to happen before they can be activated. Part IV outlines a process for discovering and activating them.

Can you summarise the three levers again, linking them with your previous concepts? For example, how do the WHY, WHAT and HOW questions fit into these three levers?

Your journey starts with passion, because it provides the fuel and sustenance for the other two levers. Passion is the answer to your WHY – why you want to do what you do.

Next, you need the right goal to give your passion direction, and something for you to achieve. The more meaningful your goal is, the more you want to achieve it. Goals answer WHAT you want to achieve.

The third lever is the *creativity* that activates your gifts and abilities. By fuelling your creativity with your passion, and aligning it to your most meaningful goal, you literally set it on fire. Identifying your gifts and abilities answers HOW you will achieve what you want.

When the three levers are turned, in the right sequence, the extraordinary happens ...

PART II
IGNITE THE HEART

One love, one heart, one destiny.

BOB MARLEY

6. LAUGH AT YOUR THOUGHTS

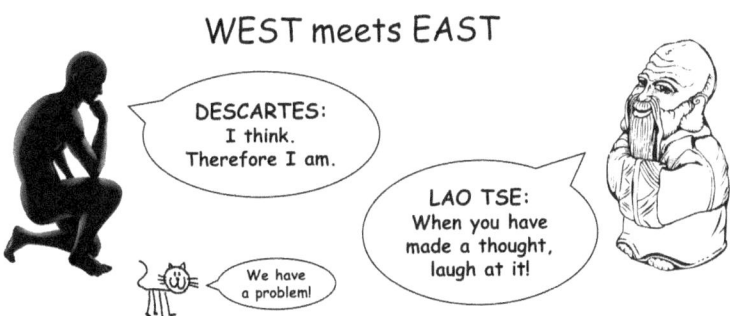

I have raised Eastern philosophy already in this book, as well as discussing the inherent difficulty in comparing Eastern and Western philosophies, because they are so different. Here is an example of what I mean.

Rene Descartes, the founder of modern Western philosophy, said: *I think, therefore I am.*

Lao Tse, the founder of Taoism, said: *As soon as you have made a thought, laugh at it.*

Where one side believes that thoughts are integral to who we are, and the other side believes thoughts are to be laughed at, a large divide exists.

You have to forgive me, but that makes no sense. At all. How can we not be our thoughts?

Simply put, that question cannot be answered in words. The answer can only be experienced, because it is unique to you and can only be fully known by you.

What this book can do is show you one way, of many possible ways, of experiencing thought*less* moments. Moments where you disassociate with your thoughts, and get a glimpse of what lies behind.

But why would I want to experience that? What is wrong with my thoughts?

Nothing is wrong, or right, with your thoughts. Experiencing thoughtlessness is a matter of choice, and depends on what you ultimately seek for yourself in life.

Do your thoughts create the person you want to be? Only you can answer that question.

In chapter 2 I raised the nature of free will, and how it works only if you have more than one choice.

Right now you only have one set of choices. Those you make with your thoughts. Experiencing thoughtlessness goes to the heart of whether you ultimately want to exercise your free will.

Because if you allow *thoughts* and *beliefs* to make all *choices*, you will never know what choices are available in their absence, and hence you cannot consider these choices.

I still don't think you have answered my question. Why would I want to have these choices?

Because moving beyond the choices dictated by your thoughts and beliefs gives you a glimpse of your true nature and essence – of the person you truly can become. It opens a doorway into your true potential, and into your inner power source – your *passion* – which changes the game.

Passion sets up the scene for you to create your own game, in which you set the rules.

In a game you have created, using your rules, you will always be successful. And how successful your game becomes depends on how much you *believe* in it, and how much *focus* you give it.

I have many questions, but, first, explain what you mean by a thoughtless reality.

A thoughtless reality is a state of altered consciousness, often experienced in meditation.

Meditation itself originates from India, with the first written records of its use dating back to 1500 BC. The process exists in one form or another in all religions, and as a concept is not controversial.

There are many types of meditation. But before describing these types, it helps to understand how meditation works.

Meditation exploits a 'limitation' in your conscious mind: *You can only focus on one thing at a time.*

You may want to reflect on this for a moment. *You can only focus on one thing at a time.*

Play with this idea in your mind. Try to think of two things simultaneously – you will notice you can't. You need to swap between them, however quickly.

It this important?

It is critical. All meditations work on this limitation, and make you focus on *something* that is *not* your thoughts.

When you focus long enough on a *non-thought*, your brain changes frequency, and you go into a slightly altered state of consciousness. Eastern philosophers call this the *no-mind* state.

The no-mind state is an important one, and it is not always fully understood. A common misunderstanding when interpreting *no-mind* is to do so literally, as in *not thinking*.

Trying to meditate by simply not thinking can make it very confusing – which, of course, involves thinking, so you end up thinking about not thinking.

In a conscious state you always have thoughts, and turning them off is impossible. Instead, meditation is about accepting your thoughts, but choosing not to look at them, not to connect with them, and hence rendering them meaningless.

This only takes place in an altered state of consciousness, because it is in this state we see that we have a *choice*, beyond what our mind sees.

Is this just a theory? Is there any science to it?

Meditation is a not about proof, or being right. It is not measurable through thinking, because it is an experience in the heart.

And even if this experience, in principle, was measurable, your experience is unique, and to measure it would require turning it into something others could relate to. Or, put differently, turning extraordinary into ordinary.

But, yes, some facts are available that may put your mind at rest.

It is well known the brain operates at different frequencies at different times:

- When your mind is active, it is in Beta state, and brainwave speed is between 12 and 38 Hertz (cycles per second).

- When your brain is in Alpha state, with brainwave speed between 8 and 12 Hertz, you are deeply relaxed, and you feel *present in the moment.*

- With your brain in the Delta state, between 0.5 and 3 Hertz, you are deeply asleep, without dreams.

- But in between the Alpha and Delta state is the Theta state, with brainwave speed between 3 and 8 Hertz. This is your dream state, and in the higher frequencies of 7 to 8 Hertz, the Theta state touches the Alpha state.

In these frequencies you are aware, but in more of a dreamlike state. It is in this state you can explore your sub- and superconscious minds, and get vital new insights about yourself and your path ahead.

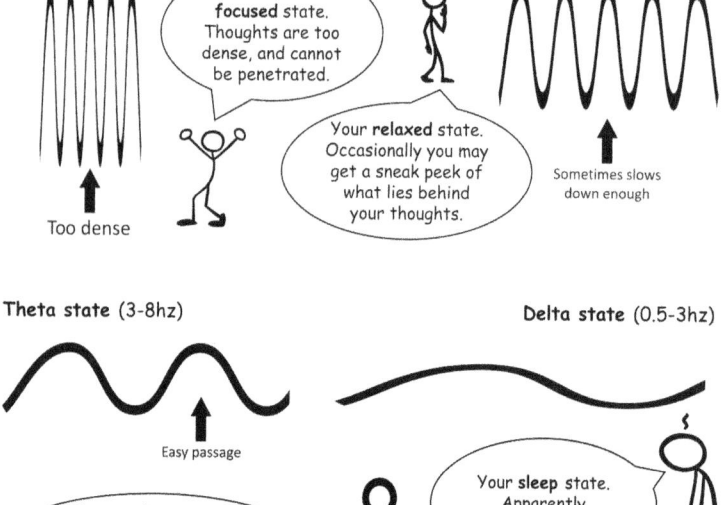

Yet these are just words. Reaching the Theta state in meditation cannot be understood by the mind, it can only be experienced though the heart.

Give me one example of how to do that. And what a 'non-thought' looks like.

You can meditate in many ways, but here is a very simple method, and one I personally like very much. It is called breath meditation, and it works by focusing on the breath.

It is ancient and very simple:

1. Breathe slowly and naturally.
2. Focus on your breath. Feel it flow into your body at the tip of your nose.
3. Maintain your attention at the tip of your nose, while you feel your breath filling up your lungs.
4. Maintain your attention at the tip of your nose, while you exhale, feeling the air leaving your lungs.
5. Feel the breath flow out of your body at the tip of your nose.
6. Repeat for at least 20 minutes.

Each time your mind wanders, and it will, go back to focusing your attention on the tip of the nose, and feeling your breath.

The mind will initially struggle with the monotony and do what it can to distract you. But if you persist, by constantly refocusing on your breath, at some stage a *click* takes place, and in that moment your experience alters.

This is a very personal experience and differs for everyone.

Can you try to describe your experience for me?

My mind typically struggles for the first 10 minutes, but I have meditated extensively. During those 10 minutes, all kinds of thoughts pop up, especially those that tell me I should get up and do something useful.

Then a *click* happens, when my brain enters the Theta state, and for me the experience is best described as *gravity* being lifted from me. I feel lighter, both in the body and mind. And thoughts look different. They no longer affect me, or try to get my attention, they simply float past.

In this place, or state, the silence is deafening because there is only me. I am still aware, I can still think, but they are not *thoughts*. I am here, but I cannot feel my body.

I love spending time in this place, floating, relaxing – just being. During this time I let go of all expectations, all wants, needs and desires.

As a result, sometimes amazing clarity hits from left field. I have achieved some of my greatest insights simply sitting in this stillness.

But I can take meditation further – much further, because once I am in my Theta state, I have choices I did not have before.

But what is most important right now is simply being able to attain the Theta state. Practise this first, by finding *your* meditation.

7. LANGUAGE OF THE HEART

Urgency vs. Importance

- What demands **most** of your attention.
- What you **have** to do.

URGENCY

IMPORTANCE

- What is most **meaningful** to you.
- What you **want** to do.

It is important you get to know the Theta state, or heart-space (introduced in chapter 6), because it's here you discover and make new and extraordinary choices.

In your heart, everything looks different.

Time ceases to exist, which dissolves the notion of *urgency*. From the ashes of urgency rises importance, giving you a new perspective of what truly matters, and what matters not.

Although each experience is unique, a common denominator of importance arises: It is something you *want* to do, versus something you *have* to do.

This is an important concept, because it connects to *values* and *beliefs*, as follows:

- When we do what we *want* to, we act from *values*.
- When we act on what we *have* to, we act from *beliefs*.

The view from each of these two points, and the subsequent results, are radically different.

Yes, that is true. I have felt the conflict many times, but I have never been able to understand it.

Your mind prioritises the *outcome*, and what you seek to *achieve*. It is forward-looking, wanting to make plans for the outcome to happen, and backward-looking, learning from past mistakes.

Your heart prioritises the *experience*, and how *meaningful* it is. It sees only one experience, the experience of *right now*. It cannot look forward or backward, and hence has no concept of an outcome.

This gives it one very interesting feature: it cannot lie. If nothing is to be gained, and being driven by what is meaningful, it makes no sense to lie.

And in that simple paragraph the heart's true power is also revealed – because if the heart cannot lie, it can only tell the truth.

And if it only tells the truth, it can be trusted.

I disagree. I know of times I have followed my heart, and it has led to pain.

We need to feel the:

- high and low
- good and bad
- exhilarating and depressing.

Because we cannot have one without the other. What would *high* mean, if there was no *low*?

Physical life has built-in obsolescence. The moment you are born, you are destined to die. All you have power over is how you choose to live your time between these two events.

> *The two most important days in your life are the day you are born and the day you find out why.*
> *—Mark Twain*

Pain is one of those things that are unavoidable in life, but it also creates an opportunity for the heart to grow and evolve. Life was never meant to be risk-free, and if it becomes so, we stop evolving as human beings.

Yet pain is not the only opportunity to grow and evolve. You can do so in many ways, including through using your *imagination* and *creativity*.

Let me now get to the point.

As your heart grows, you also grow more confident, but this is a different and new kind of confidence, less ego-based, and instead based on your inner light and passion.

You are making it sound as if the heart has all the answers. But can this really be true?

No, it doesn't. But let's view it from a different perspective.

Let's say you are at point A in life, and want to go to point B, but don't know how. What is most important?

1. To find something with all the answers?

2. To find something with the answers that you are missing?

I suggest you only need to find what you are missing, to complement what you already have, and to start something extraordinary in motion.

So what exactly is missing? I understand it is different for everyone but, to use your language, is there a common denominator?

Yes, there is, and we have already talked about it. The common denominator is the WHY question – or, rather, its absence. The answer to the WHY question makes everything else make sense, because it connects your dots.

By only addressing WHAT and HOW questions, Western society predominantly values outcome-based goals, which means you have been taught to chase a goal, achieve it, set a higher goal, and so on.

And what exactly is wrong with this?

Nothing at all. If you are alive, and living the life you truly want, you are already walking the path of the extraordinary.

But if WHAT and HOW questions don't work for you, there is another way to choose your path of the extraordinary.

This choice starts with WHY, which ultimately leads to your passion. I have been talking a bit about this already. Passion is not based on a future outcome, but on doing what you love doing, outcome or no outcome.

You haven't been taught to stop, simply enjoy the moment, and discover what this is. But doing so is essential to becoming extraordinary.

8. YOU ARE ONLY YOUR VALUES

The heart also knows something else; your **values**.

As I touch on in chapter 7, *values* are different to *beliefs*. A belief comes from the *mind*, and is a judgement and opinion of what you think is *right* or *wrong*. It takes sides.

For example, believing in one religion often precludes believing in another. Being a fan of one sports club precludes you from also being fan of a competing club. I'm sure you can think of other examples.

As a result, you have numerous different beliefs, spread across all aspects of your life.

But behind your beliefs, at the very centre of your being, are your *values*. Your values live in your *heart*, in your *soul*, and they provide your moral compass.

They are the starting point for *seeding* the extraordinary, and come *alive* when you live them.

You make it sound as if values are better than beliefs. But are they not both needed?

Absolutely.

But to make optimal use of your *beliefs*, you need to understand your *values* and, most importantly, the relationship between the two.

One piece of the puzzle is missing, and this piece will make clear this relative relationship, and what needs to come first to optimise success.

What is coming next will challenge you. Perhaps you will even be tempted to stop reading this book. But it has to challenge you, because only by being challenged do you evolve. That is human nature.

I cannot imagine what could be that controversial.

Most of your beliefs are not your own. Please read that sentence again, but slower.

They are other people's beliefs that you subconsciously choose to adopt as true.

You are right; that sounds crazy.

There is no conspiracy theory here. This is just how things have played out.

You inherit beliefs, culturally and socially, from parents, friends, school and workplace. You adopt them by osmosis, because you have never been *systematically* taught how to think outside the box.

So the answer to your question is yes – you need both beliefs and values, but only if the beliefs are your own. If your beliefs don't align with your values, they create a constant struggle.

Beliefs are about being right.
Values are about coming alive.

Let me ask you this: how many of your beliefs do you know to be your own? Truly your own? And how many of these align to your values?

I have never thought about it that way before. And I have never really thought about what my values are, other than in general terms.

Let us contrast values and beliefs by going further into how they work:

- Beliefs are simply what you *believe* to be true – for example, you believe one political party is more right than another. Beliefs are the language of the mind.

- Values are simply what you *know* to be true. You *know* when you are in love. You *know* when you are inspired. Values are the language of the heart.

But how do you tell them apart? Is there an easy way?

Yes, there is. And it is quite simple. Whatever it is you are testing, imagine it in your heart.

How do you feel? Do you feel good? Does it make you feel lighter, and more empowered? Does your heart open? Are you inspired?

Or do you feel heavier? Does your heart feel contracted? Do you feel agitated? Or out of balance?

You do what you have to because of your beliefs.
You do what you want to because of your values.

You have a choice. You can choose beliefs that make your heart close. Or you can choose beliefs that open your heart, and make you come alive.

How do I change them?

You cannot change them directly, because you do not know what they are.

But you can change them indirectly, by doing something that opens your heart.

Are you saying I need to meditate?

You can, but you also have another choice. You can do what you love doing. Or, even better, do what you love doing *most*.

Because when you do what you love doing most, you live your values, awaken your passion and come alive.

The importance of this cannot be stressed enough. Living your values and awakening your passion makes you think differently, because it redefines what is possible. This is how you change your beliefs to align with your values.

9. DO WHAT YOU LOVE DOING

To come alive is simple: do what you love doing. The more you do, the more you come alive.

Because when you do, a new energy is released, directly from your heart. Energy unlike any other.

This energy is called passion and, as I've already touched on, it is game changer.

This passion is not constricted by your mind, personality, ego, or any filter that diminishes your natural light. It is heart-matter in its purest form.

What does it do? And what makes it a game changer?

Passion resets your state from *passive* to *active*. Passive versus active state can be summarised as follows:

- In your *passive* state, you wait for things to happen and for opportunities to come to you. Life is a fixed context, which cannot be changed. It controls you and limits your choices.

- In your *active* state, you create the things you want to happen, and the opportunities you want to come your way. You are in full control of your life and its context, and your choices are limitless.

Passion redefines what is possible. It has everything it needs, and knows no limits. And because it knows no limits, it seeks nothing. And because it seeks nothing, it can achieve anything.

Can you explain what passion is in more detail – and compared to, for example, motivation?

Motivation is about keeping the mind stimulated and interested. It needs constant feeding to stay alive, because motivation is *externally* stimulated.

Passion is your *internal* and infinite energy source – and not just for you. Because your passion is limitless, it also shines for others. It is a power source that literally energises you beyond belief (pun intended).

Passion is powerful, because it knows:

- no compromise, only collaboration
- no competition, only co-creation
- no judgement, only equality
- no limits, only potential
- no fear, only courage.

Without passion, there is no extraordinary.

Perhaps this is an obvious question, but what is my passion? How do I find it? How do I know if I have found it?

Finding your passion is not that hard. Passion comes from doing what you love doing. It is that simple.

Here is a question for you to get you started: all things being equal, if you had to do *one* thing, for the *majority* of your remaining life, what would that *one* thing be?

I am not sure. It seems such a simple question, yet I haven't really thought about it.

So let's start thinking about it now. Here are some possible starting points:

- What is your hobby?
- What did you love doing as a child?
- What do you dream and fantasise about?
- What inspires you?

I find meditation a very useful tool to help answer these kinds of questions. Sometimes the mind is so busy in the day-to-day living that we need to remove ourselves all together, in order to get clarity on these kinds of questions.

But this is one of the most important things you will ever do. It is never too late to come alive, and to do extraordinary things.

Can you give an example of passion? What are you passionate about?

I am passionate about *consciousness* and *awareness*. I love communicating, exchanging ideas, pushing boundaries, challenging beliefs and connecting new dots.

What excites me in particular is the last aspect – *connecting new dots*.

Connecting dots is the source of *evolution*, because the process connects your individual pieces of inner knowing to a complete holistic picture of who you truly are, and what you are capable of doing.

The first dot is passion and doing what you love doing, because only passion holds enough energy to bring everything together.

It is hard to think that passion could be this powerful.

Yes, it is. The mind struggles with this concept. What the mind doesn't understand, it typically declares as false, and sometimes a threat.

You only have one way to find out whether passion can indeed be this powerful, and that is to do it – be courageous and take the plunge, and do something you don't fully understand, but which feels right and meaningful.

And if taking the plunge means discovering what you love doing most, and then choosing to do more of it, perhaps it is not such a plunge after all?

10. THE ART OF CHARISMA

You know how charisma feels.

You may find it hard to express in words, but when charisma is there, you feel it. Its presence, its pull, its power. Its seductiveness, in every sense of the word.

Some seem born with charisma, as if it were a second skin. They are opportunity magnets and create success. They are the people you want to know.

Having a choice of more charisma, or not, most would choose more. Do you agree?

Yes, absolutely, but I am not sure it is a choice. As you said, some are naturals at it.

Just because some seem to have it naturally, doesn't mean it cannot be learned and mastered. And, in addition, not all charisma is equal, as follows:

- The first kind of charisma is only felt in its immediacy. It attracts others, but doesn't share and doesn't ignite.
- The second kind makes ripples, and can be felt far beyond its immediacy. It empowers and ignites others.

I am not particularly interested in the first kind of charisma, or where it comes from.

Instead, this book focuses on the second kind. No-one is born with this type of charisma – it can only be mastered through practise.

It has to be this way, because this charisma is powerful. It changes things. It inspires people. It influences outcomes.

So you are saying there are two kinds of charisma? One we learn, and one other type?

Yes. One type of charisma comes from the heart; the other comes from the mind. And they work differently.

Mind-charisma comes from being *confident* in what you can do and achieve. You can replicate success at will. People are often attracted because they want that success to rub off on them too. This charisma only shines around the person who has it, and others need to compete for it.

Heart-charisma comes from being *confident* in knowing you can achieve anything that is important to you. You can re-create success at will. People are attracted because this charisma empowers and inspires them to be confident themselves, so they can create their own success. This charisma shines so brightly that it alights others.

Can you give specific examples of specific people with this type of charisma?

They are the people who make, or have made, a difference in the world – people who make a profound difference to others, whether on a small or large scale.

I often think of Nelson Mandela and Steve Jobs as examples.

Mandela mastered compassion and forgiveness during his 30-year imprisonment. The power of his heart and values, alone, prevented a civil war.

Jobs mastered his charisma through his uncompromising passion for beauty *and* technology. The power of this passion, alone, has changed how we experience technology.

Both surrendered to something bigger than themselves, which gave them the energy and impetus to achieve something extraordinary.

This is why heart-charisma is much stronger. It is unlimited because it comes from the heart. And it can be directed towards achieving anything that is congruent with your values.

Confidence. That is a big one. For many, I think.

Many are afraid, fearful of leaving their comfort zone. Although it may be a beautiful place, nothing grows in your comfort zone. Growth, and doing extraordinary things, happens on the outside.

But here is the thing. If you never try to do what you are afraid of, you will never know what you can do. You will never know your potential, and who you can become.

It's hard to do something you are afraid of. What you say makes sense, but it doesn't take away the feeling and experience of lacking confidence.

Because you think you have something to lose.

I believe the biggest thing you could lose is the experience of truly trying. To never once in life give your passion a full go, with your absolute focus and commitment, would be a terrible loss.

To live by your passion you need *courage*.

But courage requires you to *lead* with the *heart*. It requires you to open it. And expose it. And to many, that sounds frightening.

Yes, that sounds frightening. And risky. Perhaps life has enough uncertainly as it is, without adding to it?

That only holds true if you think you have something to lose. But the perceived risk is an illusion.

Your heart has no weaknesses. When you open it, it is your light that shines.

Why do I feel vulnerable when I talk about intimate things, if the heart has no weaknesses?

Vulnerability and weakness are not the same. And not all feelings come from the heart.

Your heart's vulnerability lies in its *honesty*. It knows no past or future, only the present moment, the *now*. And hence, your heart cannot lie.

Yet this is also a key strength, because honesty builds trust and authenticity, which is the first essential step in any meaningful relationship.

But we all have weaknesses, and no-one wants these exposed by being too open. If they are not in the heart, where are they?

They are in the *mind* – the subconscious mind, to be precise. And these weaknesses take the form of *beliefs*.

By now you will not be surprised when I say these beliefs are not real. They are made up – some by you, many by others. But none of them are true.

The truth is exposed when you open your heart and find you for yourself.

Can you give me an example of a made-up belief?

Why don't you give me an example of something you perceive to be a weakness?

At school, I was never good at mathematics or science, but I was very good at art.

That is a great example. You did the same tests as everyone else, including ones on mathematics, even though this is not your forte.

But being tested in something that is not your forte, and then being rated weak in that area, is a made-up thing. This rating is pointless, because you never have, and never will, work in a scientific field.

Yet it still leaves a perception of weakness within you, to this day, although it is irrelevant. Multiply this with all other ways you have been rated in life, and you begin to see the overall effect this process has on you, and your confidence.

So what do I need to do? To use your language, what is my *one new choice*?

Discover what you love doing, and do it. Commit to it.

And here is a very good reason for doing so: the difference between having no passion and having some passion, even if only 0.1 per cent extra passion, is a *quantum* difference. This holds true in both your personal and business lives. But this *quantum difference* only happens if you choose it.

How can 0.1 per cent make such difference?

Because passion, regardless of quantity, changes *beliefs*. And when you change a belief, a lot of things change.

Passion shines on what stands in its way, bringing the subconscious into the conscious, allowing you to make a new choice – in this case, a new belief.

This is how you change beliefs – by replacing old beliefs that no longer serve you with new beliefs you hand-pick.

Can you give a real-life example of this?

Let me share one of my experiences.

I have already shared my passion for *consciousness* and *connecting the dots*. For many years I thought I was unique in having my kinds of thoughts and questions – until I chose to do something with them, which was beginning to write my first book, *ON PURPOSE: The Path to Extraordinary Business Transformation*.

The passion I gained from writing this book, and the way it refined my thinking, gave me courage to introduce its principles into what I do as a management consultant.

But it was only after taking the step and introducing my new concepts to others that I realised I wasn't alone in having my kinds of thoughts.

This new insight – that many people ask similar questions of life and business – created a new belief, which now allows me to communicate authentically and powerfully.

But it starts with passion, and doing what you love doing. However little, your passion will set something big in motion.

Life is too short to not do what you love doing.

PART III
SET YOUR GOALS

A goal is a dream with a deadline.

NAPOLEON HILL

11. KNOWING YOUR ONE TRUE GOAL

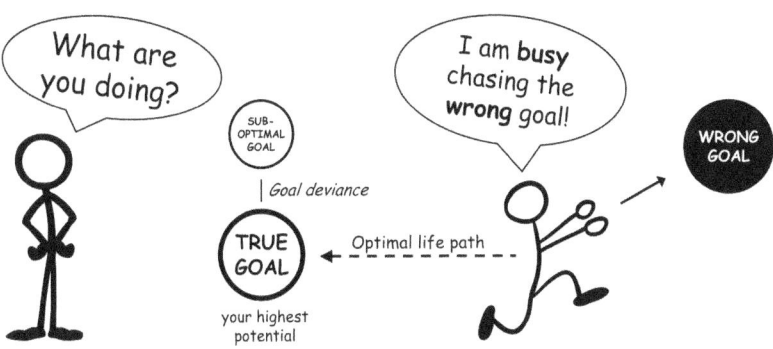

If one goal made every cell in your body tingle in anticipation, and gave you the drive and impetus to make it come true, would you want to know what it was?

Of course I would. Everyone would want such a goal. But just because it sounds good, doesn't mean it is possible.

Let's formulate a hypothesis ...

All things being equal, one goal must exist that satisfies your needs and wants more than any other goal, and holds the potential to make the greatest difference to you.

First, do you agree in principle that one goal is greater than any other goal? Even if you do not yet know yours?

Yes. It makes sense that some goals are more important than others. And, out of those, one that is most important.

This forms the basis of what I call goal-deviation theory, which can be broken down as follows:

1. Understand your one goal.
2. Understand where you are currently headed.
3. Understand the deviance between your one goal and your current direction.
4. Understand what this difference means to your life.

The difference, the goal deviation, is your deviation from your true path. Depending on its severity, this deviation will either take you closer to what makes you come alive, or it will take you further away.

How do I know what my difference and deviance is?

You don't need to. The one goal, and how to define it, is explained in the next few chapters. And once you know yours, the rest becomes obvious.

The purpose of goal-deviation theory is to highlight the supreme importance of identifying the one goal, because until you know this goal, everything will be hit and miss.

Goal-deviation theory connects with your beliefs and values:

- Your one true goal is connected to your values.
- Your current direction is connected to your beliefs.

Now we can formulate the goal-deviation theory, which states that:

> *The smaller the goal deviation, the more the current direction is aligned with the heart and values, and the more impetus and charisma are created.*

I have heard of many kinds of goals, but never goals like that.

The next four chapters outline how these goals look and work, culminating with you creating your one goal.

But before we get to that, you need to be aware of one more theory: the radar-illusion theory.

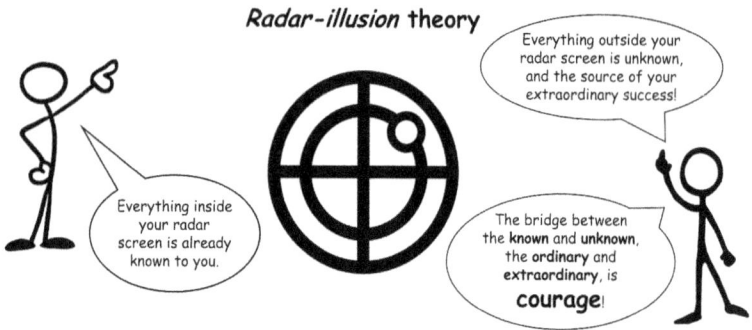

Think of the radar screen on a ship in the middle of the ocean. Anything that shows on the screen is real. Anything that doesn't exist on the screen is non-existent.

Many live their life to this theory, and plan their life according to their radar screen.

But that seems reasonable to me. How else can we plan?

Exactly. What is the choice? Discovering another choice starts with the simple question: are you happy with what is on your radar screen?

If not, the radar-illusion theory explains the problem:

Extraordinary is found outside the radar screen. It is not found in what is known, but in what is not known. Extraordinary is found in the unknown.

This highlights a potential problem. If you set your goals inside the radar screen, you limit what you can achieve. You limit your light and charisma, and your natural ability to do extraordinary things.

To be or do the extraordinary, you need to create an extraordinary goal, your one goal. And your one goal sits outside of your radar screen.

You are saying we should set goals we don't understand? And set them outside of our comfort zone?

Over the next four chapters, I cover why you only need two goals, and how that conclusion is reached.

For now, you need to think about having one goal inside *and* one goal outside of your radar screen.

Your *one* goal sits on the outside. This goal is your guiding light and source of inspiration. It doesn't change, other than getting clearer over time. It holds its own gravity, pulling you towards it.

Your *inside* goal is your *next important* goal, which I call your *next* goal. Your next goal defines what you want to achieve in the next 6 to 12 months. Once it is achieved, you formulate your next important goal.

When these two goals align, your values and beliefs are consistent, on the inner and the outer. You no longer have different *selves*, such as a work-self or a family-self; you only have one SELF that is consistent throughout all dimensions in your life.

12. UNDERSTAND GOALS AND BRAIN CHEMISTRY

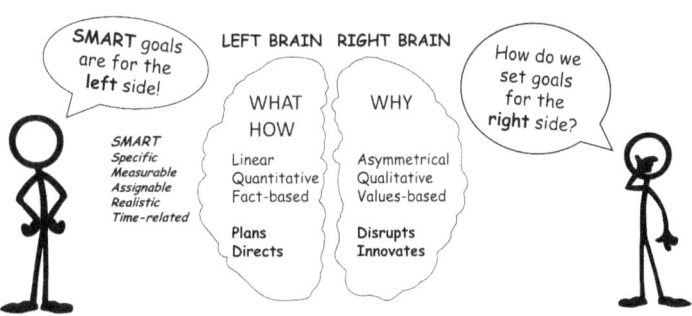

To explain the nature and essence of the two goals discussed in chapter 11 – your *one* goal and your *next* goal – I start with the brain.

The brain consists of two figurative halves that process your reality differently, yet in a complementary way.

For example, let's say you want to go on holiday. Two key activities will take place in your brain.

The left side of your brain is about *planning* and *controlling*. It is linear and relies on beliefs. Its purpose is to resolve WHAT and HOW questions. This side is what I term the *mind*.

Your mind will begin to plan your holiday, ensuring you know WHAT needs to happen, before, during and after the holiday.

The right side of your brain is about the *experiencing* and *innovating*. It pushes your boundaries. It is asymmetrical and relies on *values*. Its purpose is to resolve WHY questions. This side is what I term the *heart*.

Your heart seeks to experience a joyful and meaningful holiday.

Together these two sides co-create your reality.

> ***The intuitive mind is a sacred gift and the rational mind is a faithful servant. We have created a society that honours the servant and has forgotten the gift.* —Albert Einstein**

I can accept how the left side works, but can you please explain the right side further?

You get to know the right side, your heart, by asking WHY questions.

Yet asking WHY questions are hard, because you have never been trained in asking, or answering, them.

This is because WHY is approached with Western thinking, and that doesn't work.

Put simply: you cannot use your mind to answer questions of the heart, and expect meaningful answers.

A WHY can never be answered with a WHAT or a HOW question.

Can you give a practical example of what you mean?

Let us use the example of falling in love. This experience cannot be controlled. It cannot be quantified. It happens when it happens.

If someone were to declare their love for you, which of the following three statements speak most to your heart?

- WHAT they love about you.
- HOW much they love you.
- WHY they love you.

Well, WHY they love me. It makes it more personal, more real.

Exactly. Because WHY engages the heart. It goes to the heart of your values (pun intended).

Very funny. You said the answer to the WHY question is simple. What is my answer to my WHY question?

Anything that makes you come alive. You can find your answer in your maximum joy point.

This takes place when you do what you most love doing. Because then you live your values that awaken your passion.

It is as simple as that.

Is this related to the one goal? The one that lies outside the comfort zone?

Yes.

Your one goal is for the heart to create. This goal is intangible, and based on what makes you come alive.

Your next goal is for the mind to achieve, and to take you one step closer to your one goal. It is tangible and based on what you want to achieve in the short term.

Let's start with identifying your one goal first.

This goal needs to inspire you, and the more it inspires you, the more SEISMIC it is (more about its SEISMIC properties later).

A SEISMIC goal holds what I can best describe as a gravitational pull, because its inspiration pulls you towards it. For the rest of the book, I refer to your one goal as your SEISMIC goal, and I will explain these goals further in the next chapters.

What is your SEISMIC goal?

My SEISMIC goal is to create a new system of consciousness, available to everyone, that identifies how to truly come alive, and do extraordinary things.

I don't know of anyone who has that level of understanding of their goal.

It's a detailed understanding, but I am evolving just like everyone else, and I still don't know about many things. Yet.

But it does not matter. Understanding your SEISMIC goal is a never-ending journey, not an end point or outcome you can ever reach.

And what is your next goal?

For the rest of the book, I refer to your *next* goal as your SSMART goal. This is your next most important goal, which you plan to achieve in the next 6 to 12 months. SSMART goals are explained further in the next chapters.

For example, my SSMART goal is to complete the manuscript for the book you are currently reading.

Your SSMART goal needs to align with your SEISMIC goal. Not necessarily perfectly, but they at least need to be headed in the right direction.

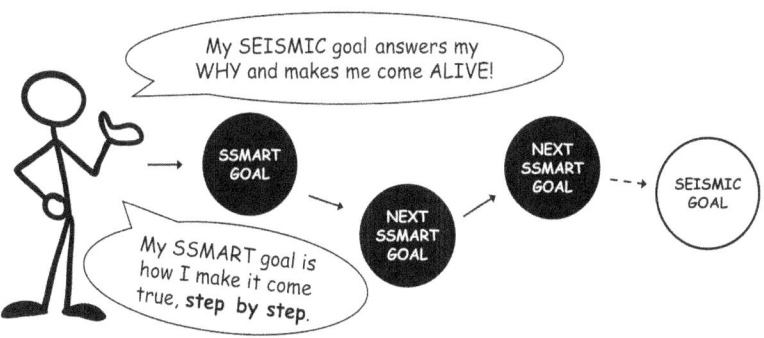

And this is where the gravitational pull becomes so important, because the more you align your SSMART and SEISMIC goals, the stronger this pull becomes.

But how do you set goals for the heart, if you cannot quantify them?

That question shows you are trying to use the *mind* to understand the heart.

The heart doesn't need to quantify anything; it simply seeks the most meaningful experience. This means its goals cannot be described in a *mind-sense*.

But they can still be described in a *heart-sense* – for example, you can set a goal based on values.

To help you with this, the next chapter introduces the SEISMIC goal-setting framework, which is designed to create goals for the heart.

13. SEISMIC GOALS THAT ROCK YOUR INNER

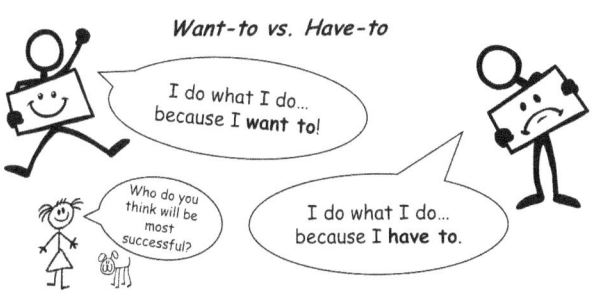

I introduced the SEISMIC goal-setting framework in my book, *ON PURPOSE: The Path to Extraordinary Business Transformation,* where I described it in the following way:

SEISMIC goal setting is a conscious approach of setting in motion breakthrough change and transformation. Because SEISMIC goals are so different to conventional goals, they drive breakthrough change because there is no incremental way of achieving them.

Although this is a business description, SEISMIC goals are clearly different. To highlight this difference, let's compare SEISMIC goals with another, commonly known goal-setting framework.

Have you heard of SMART goals?

Yes. I have used SMART goals in the past. But I can't remember what SMART stands for.

SMART stands for:

- **Specific.** What is it you want?
- **Measurable.** How will you ensure you get enough of it?
- **Assignable.** Can someone else get it for you?
- **Realistic.** How much of it can you get?
- **Time-related.** When can you get it?

These are goals for the mind. You can quantify and measure them. They are needed, but nothing in them points to something you *want* to achieve.

SEISMIC goals are for the heart, and SEISMIC stands for:

- **Soar.** How high dare you imagine?
- **Empower.** How much of your unique gifts will you use?
- **Inspire.** How much impetus does it give you?
- **Sustain.** How much does it keep you moving?

- **Meaningful.** How much difference does it make?
- **Integrate.** How does it align with your values?
- **Co-create.** How much of it can you create with others?

The rest of this chapter explains the SEISMIC goal and its properties. In the next chapter, you will create your own SEISMIC goal, as well as a tangible, SEISMIC-inspired SMART goal, called a *SSMART* goal.

SOAR

Soaring is about climbing high and seeing the big picture. This brings *clarity*.

And the biggest picture of them all is the picture of **you** – who you really are. Your full SELF, and your true potential.

Soaring is about letting go of self-limiting beliefs, so you can experience the full power of your own *light*.

EMPOWER

Empowering is when you reclaim your unique gifts and abilities – the things that only you can do.

You can consider these your *tools*, which you use with your *passion*, to achieve your SEISMIC goal. The next section of the book is about your unique gifts and abilities, and how to discover and master their use.

INSPIRE

Inspiring is about using the *strength* of your inner drive, passion and charisma.

This inner drive is the sole source of energy you need to make your SEISMIC goal come real. The goal must awaken your passion, and make you come alive.

SUSTAIN

Sustaining is about creating and maintaining a meaningful *balance* in all aspects of your life.

This is about putting everything into perspective, and seeing not only the big picture, but also everything else that affects it in a material way.

MEANINGFUL

Meaningful is about the *difference* the goal makes – not only to you, but also to others.

The more people you affect with your goal, the more critical mass the goal creates, and the greater the chance of success.

This also amplifies your charisma, because helping others become successful or extraordinary is a very strong inner feeling that makes you come alive.

INTEGRATE

Integrate is about connecting your SEISMIC and SSMART goals.

A SSMART goal is your *next most important goal*, which you plan to achieve in the next 6 to 12 months. It is your next stepping stone towards creating and achieving your SEISMIC goal.

By first knowing your SEISMIC goal, you can create a SSMART goal that resonates with both your mind and your heart.

The more you align your SEISMIC and SSMART goals, the stronger they become, the more synergy they create, and the more success they attract and manifest.

CO-CREATE

Co-create is about creating with others.

Whatever you can create and achieve on your own, you amplify when you create and achieve with others.

Imagine the world is a puzzle that consists of many pieces, and each piece is unique – no two are the same.

One of these pieces is you – you are one unique piece. And just as in a puzzle, your piece fits perfectly with some pieces, and not so well with others.

To *co-create* is to find your adjacent pieces – other people who are like-hearted and like-minded, who you can connect and create synergy with, fuelled by shared passion and values.

These are the SEISMIC attributes. In the next chapter, you will create your own.

14. CREATE YOUR SEISMIC GOAL

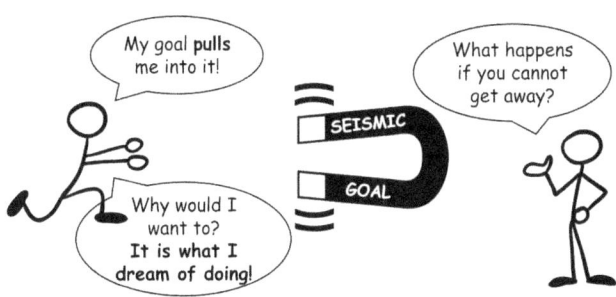

Let's begin to create your SEISMIC goal.

Soaring is not only the first of the SEISMIC attributes, but also what frames the success of the goal.

But how can we say something is successful if we cannot measure it?

What ultimately frames success is your imagination, and your actual success depends on your level of belief in it.

> *Your success is naturally unlimited;*
> *it is limited only by your mind and your beliefs.*

But didn't you say before that beliefs are less important than values?

They are equally important. And now we will expand the concept of beliefs and values yet again.

Values are your *internal* truth; beliefs are your *external* truth, and how you choose to represent your values in the outer world.

Beliefs create your *experience*, and what you manifest and attract in life. If they are not aligned to values, you manifest an experience you do not really want. This was described in chapter 1.

The importance of this cannot be understated.

Why is this so important?

The success of a goal lies in *aligning* beliefs to values. Doing so allows your heart dreams to come true, because what you believe comes true.

Can you explain again how I align my beliefs to my values?

By *soaring*. By being courageous and making a new choice - a choice to allow yourself to believe in your full SELF, and its potential.

By doing something different – something that cannot be measured, and that leads to no conceivable outcome, other than making you feel exhilarated when you do it.

Can you give me a practical example of this, perhaps using yourself?

First remember that this is *different* for everyone.

I used extensive meditation, and ultimately found my answer by asking myself this question: *what stops me from shining, and truly being myself?*

And my answer was that I was *afraid*. I was afraid of being authentic. I was afraid of speaking from my heart, both in verbal and written forms. I was afraid of being different.

To soar, for me personally, means to be *unafraid*. And to remain unafraid, and keep my heart open at all times – especially during the hard times, when all my heart wants to do is close up and retreat into the safety of its comfort zone.

That is a hard thing to do!

And that is the paradox. We are so afraid, yet we have little to be afraid of.

It may sound like a cliché, but the more you realise that you are in charge of your life experience, and your power to change and manifest different and new things, the more you realise the truth in this statement.

So what stops you from soaring? What is the core fear that stops you from taking off? And coming alive?

The answer to this question is critical, because this core fear is a key barrier to becoming extraordinary.

Okay, tell me more about gifts and abilities. I have always wanted to know what mine are.

What is more important is WHY you have them, and HOW to develop them – because until you develop them, you will not have clarity on WHAT they are.

You develop your unique gifts and abilities when you *create*, from your *passion*, for the purpose of achieving your SSMART or SEISMIC goal.

Or put differently: your unique gifts and abilities naturally develop when you create something meaningful that fulfils a higher purpose. And the more you create, the stronger they become.

Out of all the powerful concepts in this book, this one is the most powerful. Your gifts and abilities create ripples far beyond your understanding, and set things in motion beyond your comprehension.

Can you share your unique gifts and abilities?

I will share the one I use right now, which is *communication*.

More specifically, I can reduce complexity to simplicity, and effectively communicate it.

I have always been able to do this to some extent, but since I aligned my gift with my passion, and with my SSMART goal, it has been developing at light speed.

I am developing my gift right now, writing this book.

What is the next attribute?

Inspiring is your next SEISMIC dimension, and this attribute is about coming alive, fully, completely and unconditionally.

It is about being swept away with meaning and purpose, which energises and ignites every part of yourself – a bit like being in love, and looking at life through rose-coloured glasses.

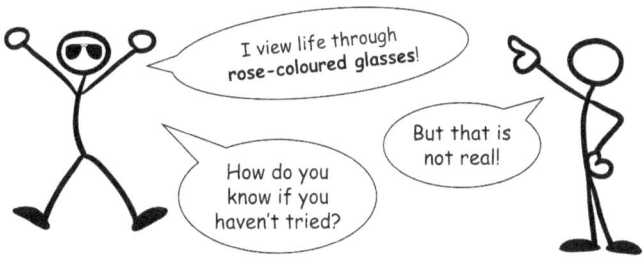

This dimension connects your goal with your passion, and gives it the *energy* and *impetus* it needs to be successful.

For example, writing this book is for me an inspiring experience that keeps me going because of the impact it has on my life, and potentially to your life.

I am a little unclear on the sustain dimension. Can you explain it further, by providing an example?

Sustain is ultimately about your *balance*.

I need to make one important distinction here: I am talking about balance, not compromise.

Balance is about understanding what you need to do to ensure your long-term journey, and this is different for everyone. We all have something that unbalances us, and that takes us off our mission.

For me, the key challenge and potential cause of imbalance is time – that is, balancing my SSMART goal with my work and family life.

To meet this challenge, I have created a routine for myself, setting aside one hour per day for writing, Monday to Friday, with five hours spread over the weekend. This is a weekly commitment of ten hours working towards my SSMART goal, which creates a good balance for me.

I am also a little unclear on the meaning dimension. Can you explain further, by providing an example?

Meaning is how your goal makes a difference, not only to yourself but also to others.

Put differently: your *gifts and abilities* are what *manifest* your goal; *meaning* is what connects it with others.

For example, what gives me extraordinary meaning is to give you a choice of coming alive. To help you connect with your inner light, and inspire you to be courageous and step into the world and shine.

The book I am writing right now is part of the *meaning* goal attribute for me.

Does it make a difference? I don't know, only you can tell.

Can you explain the integrate dimension further?

Integrate is about aligning yourself to what is most important in your life, by defining your SEISMIC-inspired SMART goal – that is, your SSMART goal.

My SSMART goal is to write the book you are now reading, as follows:

- **Specific.** I am writing a book.
- **Measurable.** I will measure it against a time-related attribute, and against my personal satisfaction measure.
- **Assignable.** I have two trusted friends who will review the manuscript for me.
- **Realistic.** I am 100 per cent committed. Time has been scheduled to allow its completion.
- **Time-related.** I will complete the written part of the manuscript by the end of August 2015.

Why do you advocate co-creating with others?

Creating on your own feels great, but co-creating with others feels even greater, and helps you create something grander than you can create on your own.

For example, I am currently creating a personal development program with two partners, based on this book. It will provide a radical acceleration of self-development, giving the participant a first-hand experience of the concepts covered in this book.

But couldn't you do that on your own too?

Why would I want to? If I am clear on what I love doing, why would I want to do something I don't love doing? Especially if I can work with someone who loves doing what I don't love doing.

For example, one of my partners is a born marketer, who loves what he does, whereas my interest is in creating and delivering conscious business and personal programs. Because we share values, we create a lot of synergy working together.

And that is the formula for successful co-creation, and for creating synergy. Creativity is optimised when everyone does what they love doing.

15. THE ART OF CLARITY

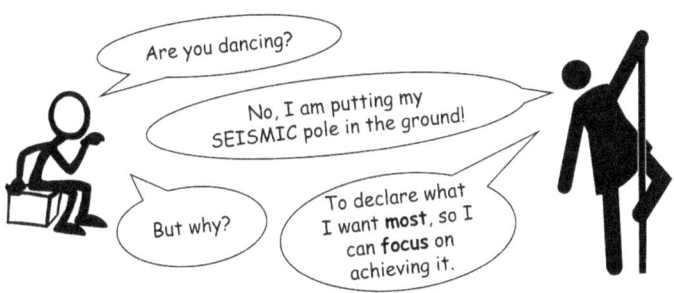

SEISMIC goals have a very important side effect.

Because they are based on what is most *important* to us, they provide a foundation from which to *relate* everything else.

What do you mean?

You live in a relative world where everything is changing faster and faster. The disruption this causes is unprecedented in human history.

But in a world where everything is changing, and uncertainty is growing, how do you manage? And, most importantly, how do you prosper?

One thing is clear. You cannot live in a world where *everything* is relative. You need a fixed point of some kind – something that doesn't change – to make sense and create meaning in your life.

Relationships and family are good examples of fixed points, and life decisions are made around these points.

Your SEISMIC goal is a fixed point – one with the added bonus of bringing a new level of clarity into your life.

What do you mean by clarity?

Clarity is seeing things for what they are, in your own context. Of course, nothing is new in this. Everyone has some level of clarity, relative to his or her fixed point and beliefs.

But this is different. For two reasons:

1. This clarity is based on what *you* believe is most important, not on external factors like family and friends.

2. When you change your fixed point, *everything* related to it also changes.

How can a SEISMIC goal change everything? Are you saying that it changes beliefs?

That is exactly what it does. To accurately define your SEISMIC goal, you must first do what you love doing and ignite your passion.

Passion creates your very own rose-coloured glasses, but not the hippie type. These ones have power. They make things happen. They attract things you don't think are possible.

They replace your most important belief about success, by replacing 'I cannot' with 'I can'. And in this process your *clarity* and *potential* changes.

Welcome to the biggest change in your life

In this new context, you no longer simply have a binary choice of right or wrong, but any shade of grey in between. By seeing the relative importance, instead of the absolute, you can prioritise your choices.

I think I am doing that already. I have many priorities in my life.

Yes. And what are they based on?

Well, according to what I have read so far, they would have to be based on my beliefs?

Yes. The problem with beliefs is that they are not good at prioritising. They are based on right and wrong, and filter out anything that is not right.

Chapter 2 describes how beliefs are formed through your upbringing, your experiences at school, in your career, with your friends and community and so on. This is inevitable and simply part of being human.

But they provide very different priorities, compared to those arising from SEISMIC clarity.

Can you explain SEISMIC clarity and how it is different?

Ask yourself: all things being equal, what one thing will bring you most clarity?

I suggest this one thing must be based on what is *most* important to you, and if you don't know what this is, you lack clarity and direction in life.

How do you use your SEISMIC goal to gain this clarity?

First, I use my SEISMIC goal to define and create what I ultimately want in life.

Second, everything is filtered through my SEISMIC goal, and it invariable emerges from this filter a different shade of grey. After this, I choose what action is most aligned with my SEISMIC goal and most meaningful.

Because this choice is based on heart rather than mind, I don't care if I am right or wrong. This means I can regularly re-prioritise, and be agile as things around me change.

This is how I attract the right people and the opportunities I want.

But this is not all. The SEISMIC goal is all about the big picture and your overall legacy, and what makes you come alive, but creating your legacy is about more than dreaming – it is also about doing.

That is why you need your SSMART goal. This sets a measurable and quantifiable goal, a step towards your SEISMIC goal, and guides day-to-day decisions.

It doesn't seem that hard! It seems we just need to look at things a bit differently, and be clear on what we want.

Yes, it is that simple. But we complicate the process, just as we complicate most other things.

To *un-complicate*, we need to use the back-to-the-dot theory – this time with an added understanding.

Your *dot* is your SEISMIC goal. And when you look at life through a SEISMIC context, it looks different.

SEISMIC goals, ultimately, are based on your *values* and, in the eyes of your values, everything looks *simple*.

You don't need to understand how something works; you only need to understand whether it's meaningful or not. And if it's not meaningful, or important, why waste moments on it?

By now you will have some understanding of your passion, and your SEISMIC and SSMART goals. As exciting as these are, they pale in comparison to the third and final puzzle piece: your unique gifts and abilities.

They don't just make you come alive. They make you come alive on steroids.

PART IV
CREATE THE EXTRAORDINARY

Creativity can solve almost any problem. The creative act, the defeat of habit by originality, overcomes everything.

GEORGE LOIS

16. THERE IS NO PLAN B

In your life, are you the **actor** or the **director**?

You've likely heard people say it's important to have a backup plan - a 'plan B' - and not to put all your eggs in one basket.

But this kind of thinking has a problem: you *divide* your focus.

Think of a magnifying glass, which can magnify the sun's rays. What will generate the most heat? Keeping energy focused on one spot, or moving it between two?

Are you saying I shouldn't have a plan B?

This is your choice. What I am pointing out is the consequence of dividing your focus.

Ultimately, it simply comes down to what you want, and how much you want it.

***The more you focus on one thing,
the more of it you attract.***

What you can achieve is unlimited – the only limits that exist are those you set for yourself. And one of the greatest limitations you can put on yourself is splitting your energy.

Because each time you split your energy, you experience less impetus, and passion dies. It may take time, but passion and the heart know no compromises.

But isn't that a bit risky? Not having a backup plan?

Even if you have a plan B, you have no guarantee it will be any more successful than plan A. The fact that it's plan B in the first place indicates you believe less in it.

New thinking and a different approach is needed.

This book began by looking at *beliefs*, and why they need to change if you want to let something new in.

The belief you need to replace in this instance is massive. It is a *core belief*, and if it's replaced, a cascade of related beliefs will also change.

It is the one belief your mind will struggle most with, because it has no context, at all, to understand what is about to follow.

But this core belief needs to be addressed, because it is the final barrier to extraordinary.

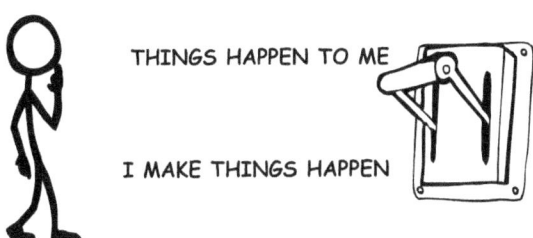

Welcome to the second biggest change in your life

The belief we need to replace is *things happen to me*. And it needs to be replaced with *I make things happen*.

But surely there are limits? I can understand we can change on the inside, but how can we change what's outside of us?

Yes, limits exist, but who sets them? And who, ultimately, decides your limit?

And here is a really scary thought: what if it is truly you, and only you? What if no limits actually exist, figuratively and literally? Other than those you make up for yourself?

That is impossible!

That is your core belief talking. By believing what you just said, you make it true. Because everything you believe comes true.

Let me share what inspires me when my mind interferes and starts telling me what is possible, and what is not.

My inspiration is the story about a black man who was imprisoned by white men for 30 years, under harsh circumstances. But instead of being consumed with rage and hate, he forced his heart open and forgave.

He practised love and forgiveness for 30 years, and this created an incredible charisma. And when this man, Nelson Mandela, stepped out of prison, he changed the world.

Was he born extraordinary? Or did he gather the courage to choose the extraordinary?

This is a good example of *making* something happen, as opposed to *waiting* for something to happen.

Do you believe everyone is capable of this?

Absolutely. It is simply a matter of choice, and courage. But remember – courage is a choice also.

Let's examine the belief just discussed: *things happen to me*. This belief holds true because you choose it. If you want to change it, you need to choose a new belief.

But how do I do that? What exactly is it I need to choose?

No direct approach is possible. You can only use the indirect approach we have already discussed. That approach starts with you regularly doing what you most love doing.

That starts to shift your belief, because as you gradually connect with your passion, you discover its power, which redefines what you think is possible.

The more you realise what you are capable of, the more you believe it and, at some point, one belief replaces another. But this time the belief is yours. You have chosen it.

This only happens, however, if you have a Plan A that gets your undivided focus and commitment.

But some limits must exist to how much we can choose plan A. People have other responsibilities also, including to others.

Of course. And this book is not for everyone.

At the beginning of this chapter, I said it comes down to what you want, and how much you want it.

You make it sound so black and white.

Because it is. Magic does not suddenly happen to you, or to me. It's not given to you, or me. You have the seed already, within you, and you can choose how much you nurture it, or how little.

Remember – there is no right or wrong. How you want to live your life, and how you want to look back at life is truly up to you.

But if you feel like I do, burning with passion, and you chose to commit to plan A only, you have a question remaining: what is plan A?

In the context of this book, plan A is anything that focuses on *creativity*, because it is creativity, and your *creative process*, which develops your unique gifts and abilities.

Your creative process is your *bridge* between your passion and your SEISMIC goal. It acts as an accelerant. The more *time* your pour into your creative process, the stronger it burns, the more it produces, and the more you evolve.

And at a speed the mind cannot comprehend.

Are you ready to put it into motion?

17. FIND WHAT IS UNIQUELY YOURS, AND ONLY YOURS

Your unique gifts and abilities are the personal and unique tools you use to achieve your SSMART goal.

You may have heard the expression 'practise makes perfect'? I like to modify it slightly – to 'practise makes extraordinary'.

The more you practise your gifts and abilities, the more they evolve. The more they shine. The stronger ripples they make. But they only develop when you choose and pursue your SSMART goal.

Okay, but what are they like? And how do I know whether or not I am already using them?

Of all the concepts in this book, explaining gifts and abilities is the hardest, because of their unique nature. Literally, no-one can do exactly what you can do. Just like no-one can do exactly what I do.

And so explaining what a unique gift or ability is poses a big problem, because I can only talk about our lowest common denominator – that is, what we both understand.

But my gift is much, much more than I can explain. And so is yours.

However, let's find common ground using the *back-to-the-dot* theory.

If we were to reduce a *unique gift and ability* to its most simplistic state, I believe it is best understood as a *massive magnifier* and *attractor of manifesting power*.

These gifts and abilities change everything. They know no limits. When passion creates and manifests a SSMART goal, you create ripples in proportions the mind cannot comprehend.

Can you give examples of people with these kinds of gifts?

All gifts are great. The question is whether you have connected with the greatness of yours, and know how to use it. In my personal experience, very few choose to discover and master their gift.

Start by looking at people who inspire you. What do they do differently? What is their gift and ability?

I admire Steve Jobs and his gift of technological understanding and vision, because I love technology and all things digital. But anyone not interested in technology may not recognise his gift in the same way I do.

So what was yours again? And can you describe how things came together for you?

In chapter 14, I shared my ability to communicate complex concepts by reducing them to their atomic simplicity, and so making the complex simple.

I have always had this gift, and I have flirted with it from time to time, but in the past I never knew how to use it systematically.

For most of my life I had thoughts, concepts and ideas circulating in my head. But because I never practised, and never let them out, they remained in my head, going around in circles, causing frustration.

Everything changed the day I decided to do something about it. I started writing, and I discovered that with every new word, sentence and paragraph, I connected new dots, and took new steps forward.

This book is a good example. It is transforming me as I write. I connect more deeply with my own gifts, and use them to connect new dots – for myself and for you.

I still don't know where to begin looking. How is a gift different to passion?

Passion is what you love doing. A gift develops when you use your passion to create your SSMART goal.

It is your act of creativity, your *creative process*, that develops your gifts and abilities.

What is your creative process?

Writing. I use writing to connect the dots about consciousness so I can explain it in a simple way. Everything I do, including my public speaking and seminars, originates from my writing.

Your creative process can be anything, as long as it creates something *new*.

This is important. It must create something *new*, because a big difference exists between creativity and *copy*.

Copy happens when you are disconnected from your passion and goal, and it isn't particularly powerful or insightful.

But many people write, so that doesn't make it unique.

But WHY, WHAT and HOW you create makes it unique, because no-one creates as you do.

This holds true for everyone. But by infusing your gift with your passion, and creating a goal that makes you come alive, you infuse your soul into what you create.

It is this uniqueness that creates ripples, and a domino effect beyond understanding.

But regardless of how talented or gifted you are, your gift can only be mastered through practise and experience, which is *repeated* use of your creativity and creative process.

And that comes from *focus*. You need to stay focused, and keep creating your SEISMIC or SSMART goal. And to do that you need a project.

18. FIND YOUR PROJECT

In chapter 9 we talked about the importance of *doing what you love doing*.

This concept will now be extended to *doing what you love creating*.

Shouldn't they be the same?

Not necessarily. Let's look at them in more detail.

What you *love doing* relates to your passion. It's what makes you come alive. It's your infinite energy source, and your source for redefining what's possible.

What you *love creating*, relates to your *inspiration*. It's what makes *others come alive*.

Can you give an example?

Let's use myself as an example.

I love reading and, in the past, I read a lot. To spend an entire Sunday reading was a norm rather than exception. But reading benefits mainly myself.

So I decided to turn my passion for reading into the creative pursuit of writing.

This transformed me from a reader into an author. The words I used to love reading, I now love writing, creating this book.

So they are related?

Yes. You must be passionate about what you create, because it is the energy source that keeps you going, especially in tough times.

And you must be *focused* and consistent – otherwise, your passion eventually dies.

And this is why you need a *project*, something that is a consistent investment in *you*, so that you can re-create yourself, evolve into your extraordinary self, and do extraordinary things.

To keep stoking the fire?

Exactly – keep your creative process alive, pulsating. Keep *creating*, on any scale, because when you create, you learn something new, and evolve.

Creativity forces evolution, because each time you expose your uniqueness to the world, you learn something new about yourself.

Creativity is concentrated personal development where you learn and master your unique gifts and abilities.

So what does a project look like?

It can be either SEISMIC or SSMART.

A SEISMIC project has (as yet) no defined outcome, and is something you do because you love it. It may be on the backburner, but it's kept alive by regular, although short, focus.

It's more of a love project, puttering along, and receiving regular attention to keep it alive.

A SSMART project is when you are serious about taking your passion and creativity into the world, and giving it enough focus to succeed.

This project needs to be a priority in your life, so that it can be achieved within the SMART guidelines – that is, within 6 to 12 months.

Writing this book is a good example.

It was a SEISMIC project for me for many years. I thought about it, played with chapter headings, and wrote bits and pieces, but didn't do anything systematic.

It only became my SSMART project in the last six months, when I felt ready to start writing it, and commit to it.

I plan the hours I spend writing, and where I write, to ensure my inspiration is the highest. And I know exactly what I need to juggle in life to make my SSMART project happen.

Can you please clarify the difference between a SEISMIC goal, and a SEISMIC project?

	GOAL	PROJECT
SEISMIC	What you want to achieve in life, above anything else.	How you keep your creative process and desire alive.
SSMART	What you want to achieve in the next 6-12 months, which takes you one step closer to your SEISMIC goal.	How you will achieve your SSMART goal, the steps to take, and how it is aligned to all priorities in your life.

A SEISMIC project adds activity to your SEISMIC goal.

A goal is ultimately an aspiration, a future state; to realise it, you need to do something. This *doing* is what the SEISMIC project adds.

Put simply, if you don't do anything, nothing happens.

What is the difference between a creative process and a SEISMIC project? From how you have described them, they sound similar.

They are. A SEISMIC project is designed to awaken the creative process.

Ultimately, everything in this book is about awakening your creative process. Passion is beautiful and powerful, but it is largely limited to those you have a direct relationship with.

Your creative process, on the other hand, creates ripples beyond your mind's understanding, and is powerful beyond belief (pun intended).

In chapter 9 I talked about passive and active states. The creative process puts you in a super active state, where you come fully alive, and where you create your purpose and destiny.

If it's this powerful, why isn't everyone doing it?

Good question. Perhaps because creativity forces you out of your comfort zone. No creativity exists inside your comfort zone, only copying and things you already know. Nothing drives and inspires you forward.

Creativity is different because it not only inspires you, but is also self-sustaining. Using your creativity, you master new things, which become new fertile creative ground, and so on.

So the reasons to start creating are very compelling? To start a SEISMIC project?

They are compelling if you have made the choice to evolve and grow your consciousness.

But I haven't spoken about the biggest benefit yet.

The creative process sets you free!

It allows you to play *your* game, not someone else's. In your game, you set the rules – and change them, when it suits you.

You are probably already playing your own game in your mind, with thoughts such as:

- *If this were me, I would ...*
- *Why don't they do this instead ...*
- *If only I could ...*

With your new understanding, you can apply back-to-the-dot theory and ask the question: WHY is this important?

Because creativity, your creative process, connects your inner game with the outer world, and makes it real.

Creativity opens the door to manifesting powers that change everything. When you connect with these, things are never the same again ...

19. GET SHIT DONE

Get shit done means go out and create.

Don't think about it, don't plan it, don't prepare for it, don't talk about it. Go out and do it. Make it a habit, starting now.

Just like that?

Yes, just like that.

Preparation is critical, but you have already done that. That was the previous 18 chapters. What's needed now is **action**.

Again, we can compare this to taking a holiday or travelling. You have done your research, identified your destinations, and booked all your travel and accommodation. But you are still sitting behind your computer at home.

This is the crossroad you face. You can stay in the comfort of the inner world and its dreams, or you can step into the outer world, and make those dreams real.

If I understand you right, we do this by creating something new?

Exactly.

This goes to the heart of success. And it's simple.

The more of your inner world you share with the outer world, the more you attract it.

This is why preparation is so important – to ensure you attract what you want. To be clear on WHAT you want to attract, you need to be clear on WHY you want it.

Yet once you are clear on your WHY, your preparation is complete.

Next we turn to your WHAT and HOW, your manifesting processes, to give your creative process form.

This becomes your production line, where you manufacture regular creativity.

Or, put simply, your creative process is used to produce creative output.

Produce output? **It sounds a bit machine-like. Surely quality is more important than quantity?**

What does quality mean if the quantity is zero?

Quantity gives meaning to quality, just as quality gives meaning to quantity. They are both important; you simply need to approach them in the optimal order.

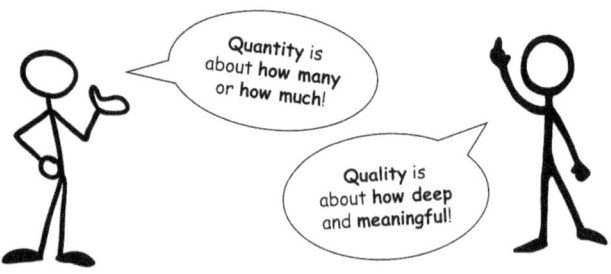

Let's explain it somewhat differently: quality is simply a proxy for WHY, and quantity is a proxy for WHAT and HOW.

And why is this important?

Because your potential for success can loosely be mathematically expressed as quality × quantity.

This means once you are clear on your WHY, you can switch your focus to your WHAT and HOW, because this is how you manifest.

So is it really a question of how much we can create? How much we can produce?

It truly is. And would you want it to be any different? Isn't creating and doing what you love doing the ideal combination?

Putting it in reverse, of course, means that you cannot keep producing if you haven't connected with your passion.

I am an artist. Does that mean I should paint and produce as much as possible?

If you want to get your art known, absolutely. How else will people know about it? How many famous artists do you know who only produced a few works?

But that is not the real reason. The real reason you should produce as much as possible is because the more you paint, the better at it you get, and the more you can *differentiate* - that is, *shine your own uniqueness*.

So this is not a production line and numbers game simply focused on producing units, producing more also fuels the evolution of your creative process and unique gifts and abilities.

And, in your case, your growth as an artist and as a human being.

What do you do? Are you focused only on writing this book? Or do you have other, supporting activities going on also?

I do. And what I focus on comes down to the discussion in chapter 12 about the left and right side of the brain.

If I favoured the left side, the outcome, I would almost exclusively focus on writing this book. And I would make choices to focus on the book, regardless of how I felt.

But I favour the journey, and the feeling of my creative process being alive and firing. And this feeling is strongest when it is uncontrolled – which means my creative process can take me anywhere.

Most of the time my creative process takes me to writing this book. If it didn't, it would be the wrong SSMART goal.

But sometimes it doesn't, and then I write other things, such as my LinkedIn blog, or an article for a magazine. Or any other writing that is public, such as industry blogs and magazines that support my SEISMIC or SSMART goals.

Don't you get distracted when you have many things going on around you?

How much you allow yourself to be distracted depends on how far you have resolved your WHY, and understand your core values.

Your WHY connects your dots.

Let me explain using myself as an example.

I use the *back-to-the-dot* theory on everything I do. My dot is to create systems of consciousness that *make us come alive.*

This means that if don't feel like writing my book, and instead write a blog article, I know they will be connected – for example, what I post on LinkedIn often ends up in this book, or in one of my keynote presentations, or even in a new sales pitch.

But here is the thing. Everything is connected, which means our most precious resource, time, is maximised. And more time allows longer focus, and longer focus makes an extraordinary difference.

Now you have all the pieces of the puzzle. In the next and final chapter, you will connect the pieces into a simple framework for being and doing the extraordinary.

20. THE ART OF MANIFESTATION

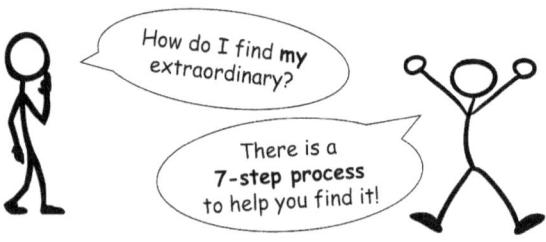

We have talked about a number of concepts so far, and the time has come to connect everything. And that will be easy, because everything originates from the same dot.

So what's the dot?

Your SEISMIC goal – your optimal end state, where you are fully alive, and fully empowered to make extraordinary choices. Your natural state of genius.

This cannot be described, because it is unique. But we can describe the journey. Using back-to-the-dot theory, we can summarise the concepts presented in this book into a seven-step process.

STEP 1: FIND YOUR PASSION

The process begins by ensuring you have enough energy. This is a critical success factor in any endeavour. Without food, the athlete goes nowhere. Without petrol, the car goes nowhere.

The energy needed to make you come alive is passion, which comes from doing what you love doing most.

Does the process have to start here? Can I set my goals first?

To define your SEISMIC goal you need to know your passion and values, because these relate to specific SEISMIC goal attributes.

So you could set your goal first, but by focusing on discovering your true *love of doing* in life, your passion, you will get a head start on all goal attributes.

So it must start with passion?

It cannot start anywhere else, because without energy, you have no impetus for action or change. And when you connect with your passion, feel it beating in your heart, your view of yourself, and what you are capable of, radically changes.

This evolved and expanded view of yourself is critical in your SEISMIC goal-setting, and in your creative process.

STEP 2: BE CLEAR ON YOUR VALUES

The second step in the process is to be clear on what is *most important* and *meaningful* to you, which are your values. This is important, because knowing and living your values goes to the heart of authenticity and trust.

Knowing your passion is a starting point for identifying your values – values and passion are connected, because they come from the same source, your heart.

When you live your passion, some things become extra important to you, and these things point to your values.

Start using them. Make them as real as possible. When someone asks what you do, don't reply with a job description; instead frame your answer around SEISMIC or SSMART attributes, as follows:

- **Values-based introduction:** I believe everyone should have the choice of being extraordinary, and I am writing a book explaining how everyone can choose it.

- **Passion-based introduction:** I am passionate about helping people be and do extraordinary things, and I am writing a book explaining how everyone can.

- **SSMART-based introduction:** I am writing a book about how to come alive, and be and do extraordinary things.

- **SEISMIC-based introduction:** I am writing a book about higher consciousness, including a blueprint for raising the overall humanity of mankind.

For example, if someone asks me in a work setting what I do, I say *I am passionate about transforming businesses and business leaders from ordinary to extraordinary.*

Can you give an example of one of your values?

My passion is communicating, in writing or verbally.

But what do I communicate? I communicate about consciousness. And what values underpin consciousness?

In my view, one of the values underpinning consciousness is truth. And that is one value I live fully in my life, with zero tolerance for deviance. At home. At work. In my relationship. With my friends.

It doesn't mean I expect truth from others, or that I always choose to communicate my truth. But I am always truthful to myself, and I never knowingly communicate any untruths.

STEP 3: DEFINE YOUR SEISMIC GOAL

A SEISMIC goal is the greatest goal you can imagine. All things being equal, it is the one thing you want to achieve most in life.

The importance of this goal cannot be understated. The more clarity you have on your SEISMIC goal, the more gravity it will have, and the more impetus and direction it will create.

How does this work in real life? How does it work for you?

Once I was clear on my SEISMIC goal, *create systems of consciousness that make us come alive*, I set the intention to realign my career, and find the perfect role to make this possible, and get it out into the public.

STEP 4: DEFINE YOUR SSMART GOAL

Your SEISMIC-inspired SMART goal is an important and meaningful goal to be achieved in the next 6 to 12 months. This sets the exact target, so you can focus your intention and energy.

A SEISMIC goal remains an unrealised dream unless you ground it, which is the purpose of your SSMART goals. They ground your SEISMIC goal, bit by bit, and progressively build your legacy.

What was your previous SSMART goal? Before writing this book?

To manifest a job that supported my SEISMIC goal, and gave me access to people or groups of people where I could make most difference.

I am a management consultant and advise CEOs of medium-sized corporations on digital disruption and its business impact, challenges and opportunities, and what different and new thinking is needed to meet it.
This goes to the heart of my goal, because many of my systems are about changing thinking – such as this book.

STEP 5: DISCOVER YOUR UNIQUE GIFTS AND ABILITIES

Discovering your unique gifts and abilities happens when you know your passion and your SEISMIC goal, and you make the choice to use your passion to create something that aligns to your goal.

The quickest way to discover your gifts and abilities is to commit to a SSMART goal.

What new clarity and insights have you received on your gifts and abilities, as part of your previous and current SSMART goals? Are they similar?

They are different. My previous SSMART goal gave me greater clarity on how to manifest what I want, and how to set powerful intentions.

My current SSMART goal gives me greater clarity on how to simplify complexity.

STEP 6: GET SHIT DONE

The sixth step is to get shit done. The more you focus and commit, the more you achieve.

This is not a linear relationship – while it starts out linear, as you focus and commit, your achievements take more of an exponential direction.

How does this work?

Because *doing* closes the loop.

It's the final piece in the puzzle. In chapter 10 we talked about *charisma*, and in chapter 15 about *clarity*.

Your charisma is your personal power, and your clarity is how you see and prioritise what is most important.

And together they created all the synergy they needed.

When these two come together you set up your creative production line, your export machine of uniqueness, programmed to make a difference the way you know best.

Do you know what your next SSMART goal is?

Yes. After this, I will write my next book, which is about creating a fully digital enterprise business, addressing both the new *thinking* and *doing* needed for successful transformation.

STEP 7: JUST DO IT

The seventh step is **just do it**.

The catalyst and accelerant to start anything is *courage*.

Courage is deciding to *make* things happen, rather than *letting* things happen. It's what flips the dominos, and sets in motion things that cannot be understood by your mind.

It makes your heart and soul jump with joy, in anticipation of fulfilling its life purpose and realising its highest potential.

Extraordinary is always only one choice away.

Is it yours?

CONCLUSION

Do what you love doing. Find your true goals. Create your dreams. It's as simple as that.

But I have two more concepts to introduce. When these come together, they create the final step, so that you can take your extraordinary to its most extraordinary level: **the sum of all your extraordinary**.

Mathematically, it is proven that the sum of infinity is greater than any one infinity itself. Extraordinary works the same way.

The sum of all your extraordinary is your ceiling – your limit, physically, mentally, in mind, heart, spirit and soul. Whatever word you can think of.

And what is it? How is it different to what you have described so far?

It is different in two important ways.

Firstly, the *sum of your extraordinary* is the outer boundary of your *imagination*. You cannot become, you cannot think, and you cannot do, what you cannot imagine.

Imagining is not dreaming. It is practising opening your heart.

Now, having read the full book, you know that an open heart is the beginning of redefining what is possible, and that no limits exist here – other than those you set for yourself.

Okay, and what is the second difference?

This difference involves two new concepts, and a new theory – the *nothing-something-everything* theory.

This theory states that you have two choices, and that these two choices each create a *quantum shift* in your life.

The first choice, the choice from *nothing* to *something*, has already been touched on. As we discussed in chapter 10, this is the difference between nothing and 0.1 per cent.

Going from *nothing* to *something*, regardless of how small that something is, is still *infinite*. And this is why it creates a quantum shift.

Are you saying that 0.1 per cent or 99.9 per cent of something are the same? And makes no difference?

They are not the same. But whereas the growth from nothing to 0.1 per cent is infinitely exponential, the growth from 0.1 per cent to 99.9 per cent is linear.

The growth from 99.9 per cent to everything (100 per cent) is also infinitely exponential, but with one critical exception: it has no limits.

It doesn't end, because everything is infinite.

What do you mean it doesn't end? Our abilities have limits, as does our potential.

How do you know that? Do you know that to be absolutely true? Have you given anything 100 per cent, absolutely everything, and proven that to yourself?

I say the opposite is true. At 100 per cent, it is not a question of *limits*, and the limited, but of the unlimited.

And this raises an interesting conundrum. If you can manifest anything, what happens if you manifest the *wrong* thing?

In a world where you have 100 per cent of everything you want, what do you want?

I have never thought about it. But why think about it, if I cannot have it?

What if you cannot have it, because you haven't thought of it?

You cannot choose what you don't know. What if you make it true, simply by believing it?

You've likely heard the old expression, 'Be careful what you wish for'. At 100 per cent, you don't operate at normal human speed. Everything is amplified, which is why you need to be clear on what you truly want – a lack of clarity could cause devastating results.

And this takes us to the conclusion of this book, and to the final theory, the *sum of extraordinary* theory, which connects the final dots.

CONCLUSION

> ***The sum of extraordinary = your full potential = (SEISMIC creativity)$^{100\%}$.***

I am not religious, but one verse from the Bible has made a great impression on me, and I am going to use it to connect the *final* dot of this book.

> ***So God created mankind in his own image, in the image of God he created them; male and female he created them. —Genesis 1:27***

To me, God is only a name – it could just as well be Spirit or Universe. What is important is not its name, but its purpose.

What is its purpose?

To *create*. I believe God is best understood as the **Creator**.

Now it gets interesting. If the Creator created us in its image, you and I are also creators.

This is the final dot. **Your creative power is God-like**. It knows no limits or barriers. It is unbounded, in the truest sense, limited only by your imagination.

You unleash it through the *sum of extraordinary* theory. And once unleashed, it is the most intoxicating power of all; the power to make a real difference to yourself and others.

What are you waiting for?

www.ingramcontent.com/pod-product-compliance
Lightning Source LLC
Chambersburg PA
CBHW070623300426
44113CB00010B/1628